Form
Letters

**Fill-in-the-blank notes
to say anything to anyone**

Form
Letters
Laura
Olin

Abrams Image, New York

Editor: Samantha Weiner
Designer: Devin Grosz
Production Manager: True Sims

Library of Congress Control Number: 2015955307

ISBN: 978-1-4197-2218-9

Printed and bound in the United States
10 9 8 7 6 5 4 3 2 1

Abrams Image books are available at special discounts when
purchased in quantity for premiums and promotions as well
as fundraising or educational use. Special editions can also
be created to specification. For details, contact specialsales@
abramsbooks.com or the address below.

ABRAMS The Art of Books
115 West 18th Street, New York, NY 10011
abramsbooks.com

Contents

For James,

who writes the best letters.

To you, the person reading this

Please write in, tear out pages from, and generally use the crap out of this book. (Important note: Only after you've bought it.)

SUGGESTED STEPS FOR USE

1. Choose a letter—anything from a letter to your crush to a letter to the person who's cutting their nails in a public place (WHY?!).

2. Fill in the blanks provided to make the letter yours.

3. Tear it out or take a photo to share it with someone.

4. Enjoy their response.

5. Repeat.

You can share your own letter or check out other people's letters with the hashtag #formletters, anywhere hashtags are served.

Have fun,
LO

To romantic partners (hoped-for or actual)

_____,

So maybe you remember that I came up to you last _____
at that _____.

I said that I had kinda _____ you for years, and thought
you were _____ and incredibly _____.

You said _____. And you were
a bit _____ about it.

And I just wanted to say: It's cool. It's cool because I know a few
things you don't:

For one, I am _____.

I am _____, _____, and _____.

I'm also _____ as hell. As *hell*.

I just wanted to let you know all that so if we run into each other
at another _____, it doesn't have to be awkward.

I'll say hi if I'm with my new _____.

_____

TO YOUR ONE-NIGHT STAND

Hey, you! You may notice that I'm not in your bed anymore!

Just to save you some wondering, I am, in fact, nowhere to be found in your apartment!

There are good reason(s) for this!

CHECK ALL THAT APPLY

⬭ I have forgotten your name, and I am embarrassed!

⬭ I don't usually do this sort of thing—have relations with near-strangers—and it seems less socially awkward to leave before you're awake!

⬭ I have an early appointment this morning! (A real one!)

⬭ I have an early appointment this morning! (A fake one I am making up to spare your feelings!)

⬭ Anyway, you seem very nice, thanks for not murdering me in my sleep, and maybe see you around sometime!

_____

I have so many questions.

TO THE PERSON YOU WANT TO TURN DOWN GENTLY

_____,

I'm so flattered that you _____ me to _____.

I _____ you so much, but I want to be up front with you:
I don't _____ you in that way.

I hope we're _____, or will be soon.

Let me know when you want to _____.

_____

Hey [   ],

Do you know about read receipts?

Love,

[   ]

_____ ,

Could you please come over
now-ish to help me

CHECK ALL THAT APPLY

◯ sort out emotional baggage about my ex

◯ get a bat in my attic—no, I don't know
   how it got in there

◯ finish this ice cream

(This is a booty call.)

Sincerely,

_____

Dear _____,

I love you this much:

Put your pen here*

*AND START DRAWING AN ARROW TO THE RIGHT.
CONTINUE FOR AS MANY PAGES AS YOU WANT . . .

TO THE PERSON YOU LOVE

[   ],

Do you like me?

FEEL FREE TO CHECK ALL THAT APPLY AND RETURN TO SENDER

- [ ] Yes!
- [ ] No.
- [ ] Maybe.
- [ ] It's complicated.
- [ ] I like you but I'm not sure I *like* like you.
- [ ] Ask me again after this next drink.
- [ ] Who are you again?
- [ ] [   ]

[   ]

Hi _____,

I've been thinking a lot about us and what happened when we
_____.

You may not have realized this, but I was _____ in love
with you. Maybe you did know it. Anyway, I just wanted to say
thanks for not being in love with me back.

Back then, if you had loved me back, I wouldn't have
_____.

Maybe I wouldn't have learned to _____.

Maybe I wouldn't have moved to _____.

I probably wouldn't have met _____.

At the time, it sucked so much that you didn't _____ me
the way I _____ you.

But now I am pretty grateful.

So thanks for not _____ —
it's one of the best things that ever happened to me.

_____

TO THE EX WHOSE INSTAGRAM YOU ARE STALKING AND WHOSE VERY OLD PHOTO YOU HAVE ACCIDENTALLY LIKED, THEN UNLIKED OUT OF PANIC, THEN LIKED AGAIN AFTER REALIZING THAT THEY PROBABLY ALREADY GOT THE NOTIFICATION

_____,

Did you hear about this weird Instagram bug where people's really old photos are getting liked by people in their follower list? Particularly the photos with their new [girl/boy]friends?

Weird, right?

Anyway, just so you know.

_____

_____,

Before you, I never missed people, really.

I mean, I missed my _____ when I was away at _____ and _____ when we hadn't seen each other in a while.

But the kind of missing you hear about in pop songs and poetry—that was totally _____ to me. I guess I didn't know before you that home can be a person.

All this is just to say—I miss you.

_____

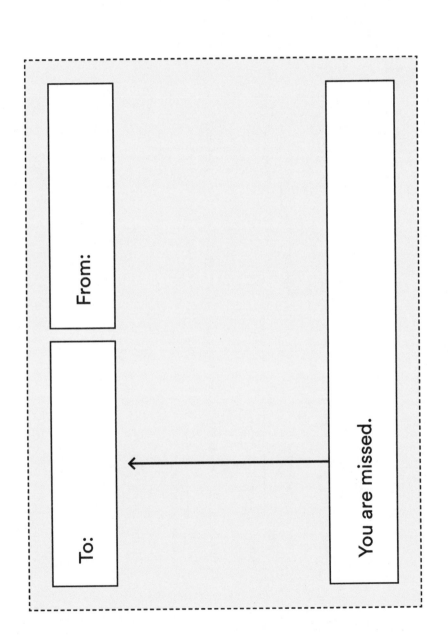

From:

To:

You are missed.

[_____],

I'm probably not going to change.

You are [_____]

[_____]

[_____] to keep trying.

Love,

[_____]

TO THE FRIEND YOU ACCIDENTALLY
(BUT NOT REALLY ACCIDENTALLY)
SLEPT WITH LAST NIGHT

Hey _____,

So, that happened.

And before we fall all over each other to claim it was a mistake,
I just want to say right away:

It didn't feel like a mistake to me.

You are hot and I like you. Like, I *like* like you.

How do you feel about me?

_____

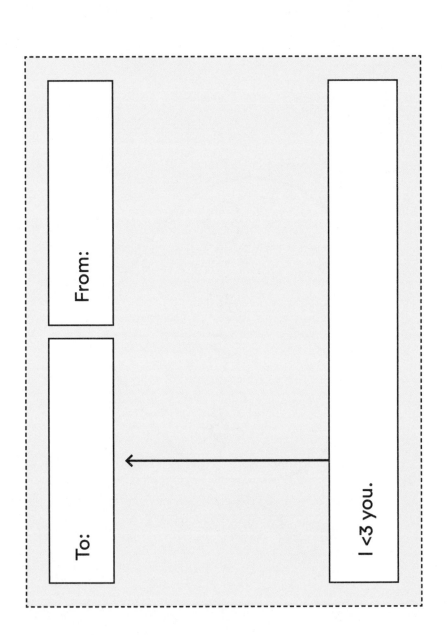

Hey _____,

So we've known each other for a while now.

_____, in fact.

And we're _____ friends,
and we have a lot of fun together.

And I think we should _____.

There are these moments when I'm _____ about it and
I can tell you're _____ about it too.

But we never do.

I bet the next time we see each other, we'll have a _____
_____ time looking each other in the eyes.

But I think it might be worth it.

Right?

_____

MISSED CONNECTION

To the _____ at _____ on _____,
around __ __ : __ __ [am/pm]:

I was the _____ with the _____ who _____
_____.

I think you're really _____.

Want to plan to run into each other on purpose this time?

_____,

_____

                        ,

I'm probably not going to change.

It's not   , it's   .

               ,

_____,

I'm heading to _____
for _____, which
means that soon a _____ will carry me
far away from you.

I regret that fact, but I also promise that this
is a goodbye-for-now and not a farewell-
forever.

See you soon.

_____,

_____

To yourself

I will _____

_____.

I will not _____

_____

_____.

I care more about _____

than _____ .

The goal is _____

_____

_____.

There is no other goal.

Remember to [   ]

[   ]

[   ] .

TO YOU, TEN YEARS AGO

Hi, former me,

If I recall correctly—and I'm getting old, so maybe not:

You're living in _____ right now with _____.

You're working _____ and you feel _____ about it. Most of the time.

With your days off you usually _____ with _____.

Life's pretty _____.

But here's what I wish I—you—had known then:

Don't get involved with _____. It'll turn out _____ and you'll feel _____ about it.

Ask _____ to be your [friend/girlfriend/boyfriend/mentor] way earlier than you did.

Buy stock in Apple.

You're going to be fine.

See you soon,

_____

Dear future me,

You're judging me, I know.

You wish I'd been smarter, _____, and _____.

Why did I _____ when it was obvious
I should have _____, instead?

Here's what I was doing:

The best I could with the _____
_____ that I had at the time.

If you talk to you (me) ten years from your now, you can tell you
(me) the same thing.

Give us a _____ break. We _____ deserve it.

Love,

_____

I will never be [   ].

To family

Hi, family!

Let's get a few things out of the way.

Yeah, I've gotten older! ___ ___ years old this year.

I'm a _____ in _____.

Thanks for asking about my love life!

I'm currently _____.

I think we're all caught up on me now. What about you?

Love,

_____

USE THIS SPACE TO WRITE A LETTER TO YOUR MOM.

If you're stumped, you could just say "I love you."

USE THIS SPACE TO WRITE A LETTER TO YOUR DAD.

If you're stumped, you can ask him what to get him for his birthday that's not another tie. (And don't forget to say "I love you.")

Dear _____,

When you are very, very old—possibly even as old as I am—and have kids of your own, you will understand something about parenthood:

It is completely freaking terrifying.

Someone—maybe it was Ralph Waldo Emerson, or else Steve Jobs—said that having kids is like having your heart walking around outside of your body.

So maybe you understand why I want to give my heart a curfew sometimes, and give it lectures about not getting into cars with drivers who have been drinking, and make sure its eyes don't get irrevocably screwed up by the newest virtual-reality headset.

I'm pretty selfish about my heart and its welfare.

I hope you understand, but if you don't, that's OK.

You still have to be home by eleven.

Love,

_____

_____,

In case there's a chance it'll change your behavior, I just want you to know that _____ refer(s) to you as "the sketchy uncle."

Love,

_____

USE THIS SPACE TO WRITE DOWN A LIST OF QUESTIONS YOU
WANT TO ASK YOUR GRANDMOTHER, GRANDFATHER, OR BOTH.

Examples: How did they meet? What was it like for them growing
up? What's been the happiest moment of their lives so far? The
saddest? The most surprising? What do they wish they'd known
when they were your age? Then ask them these questions the
next time you see them. Stories are better in person.

I am disturbed by how attractive I find you.

TO YOUR NEW NEPHEW OR NIECE

Hey _____,

It's _____. Or, as you will come to know me, your cool [uncle/aunt].

I just want to make sure you know you can come to me for a specific set of things:

- Sympathy when your parents are being annoying.
  (Hi _____.)

- Advice, when you need it.

- A slightly less-awkward version of the sex talk, when you need it.

- Ice cream your parents don't want you to have, because spoiling you is my sacred right and duty as the cool [uncle/aunt].

- _____

- Anything else you need.

Welcome to the family, kid.

_____

_____,

Just for the record:

You were wrong about _____.

I was wrong about _____.

I still think you're _____.

Love,

_____

_____ ,

What are you planning?

You can tell me.

_____

[_____],

Who's a good dog?

Who's a good dog?

Yeah, who's a good dog?

[_____] is a good dog.

You're right, buddy.

That's you.

[_____]

TO THE YOUNGER SIBLING WHO MAYBE DESERVES SOME TAUNTING

I am _____ and

you are not _____.

To friends

Hey_____,

PICK YOUR POISON

◯ booze

◯ ice cream

◯ puppies

◯ a bong (in the states and municipalities where strictly legal, of course)

◯ a dartboard with his/her face on it

◯ subtle internet revenge of some kind, like gaming search results so that their name brings up: "Did you mean 'sociopath and terrible kisser'?"

◯ all of the above

Now, name a time for me to show up at your door:
__ __ : __ __ [am/pm]

And I'll see you soon.

_____

TO SOMEONE WHO WORKED REALLY HARD ON SOMETHING AND FAILED

Hey _____,

When we are old and sitting on the front porch of a _____ somewhere, here is something we will never say: "I wish I tried less."

(Who would want to sit on the porch of a _____ with someone who said things like that? Not me.)

I'm really sorry that _____ didn't work out. I am _____ proud of you for giving it your all.

By the way, let's also be friends until we're __ __ __.

Love,

_____

_____,

Holy _____, you're really doing it. On this _____ occasion, it seems worth pointing out a few things:

That time we were at _____ after your breakup with _____ and you _____ that you would "never get married" and I said, "You'll meet someone _____ someday."

The point I am making here is that I was right and you were wrong.

Your first date with _____ at _____, after which you said _____ and I said _____ .

The point I am making there is that I was right and you were wrong.

But the most important thing here is that you found a great _____, and I am so _____ for you, because I know you'll be _____ happy for a really long time.

And as you know, I am usually right.

Love,

_____

TO SOMEONE WHO'S HAVING A BABY

Hey _____,

OMG I just heard you're having a baby!

I just wanted to say congratulations, and also to remind you that a baby is basically an alien parasite that is going to be inhabiting [your/your partner's] guts for nine months.

Just think, everything [you/your partner] eat[s] is going to be turned into baby _____, baby _____, and tiny, creepy baby reptile teeth.

Your bundle of joy is going to hear and be affected by everything you do over the next nine months, including _____ and _____.

Everything.

And as we speak, it's a little mutant _____ not remotely resembling the shape of a person.

Anyway, I'm so _____ for you and I can't wait for the shower.

Love, _____

_____,

OMG, you _____ a new person!

I want to offer my services for the following:

CHECK ALL THAT APPLY

☐ Cooing indecipherable words at your baby.

☐ Telling you your baby is really adorable when [he/she] still looks like a tiny, wizened _____.

☐ Playing hour-long games of peek-a-boo with your baby when you are too goddamn sick of peek-a-boo to do it and just want to take a goddamn shower.

☐ Coming over to your place on a Saturday night to watch Netflix and drink wine on your couch, because you can't find a babysitter.

☐ Smiling and nodding as you take fifteen minutes to recount _____'s newly acquired fine motor skill. But fifteen minutes is the upper limit.

These offers are good for this kid and may continue to be redeemable upon the arrival of another, but let's talk if you get to three.

Love, _____

_____ ,

Here are some true things:

Just because a relationship didn't last forever, it doesn't mean it was a failure.

You are _____ without _____ .

You've got a lot of people who love you in your corner. Including me.

Love,

_____

You know you don't have to

marry them all, right?

_____,

Think for a second about all of _____'s favorite things:

Some _____ with dinner. A trip to _____. That _____ toy. More _____.

If there is a _____ heaven I bet _____ is there right now, and so happy because [he/she] is getting all those things every day. Without getting fat. _____ heaven is great.

Thinking of you.

Love,

_____

Hey _____,

Here are things a job is not:

- a measure of your worth as a person
- a reason that people are friends with you
  (if they are really worthy of being your friends)
- a family
- your whole future

Getting _____ sucks, but I just want to make sure you remember all the stuff that doesn't suck.

_____ me if you want to _____
_____ tonight.

Love, _____

TO SOMEONE WHO IS GRADUATING (PRESCHOOL)

Hey _____,

You did it! You graduated from _____!

Now, it is customary for everyone you know, including your
_____, to give you Life Advice.

So here's my go:

Remember that the world owes you nothing, except maybe crayons.

Be humble, especially when learning how to _____.

The alphabet might have been tough, but _____
will be even harder. If you get overwhelmed, just remember to take
it one day at a time.

Pet all the dogs you can, but maybe skip the ones that are
significantly bigger than you.

You're going to be great.

_____

Hey _____,

You did it! You graduated from _____!

Now, it is customary for everyone you know, including your
_____, to give you Life Advice.

So here's my go:

Remember that the world owes you nothing, except maybe an
adequate supply of oxygen.

Be humble, especially when _____.

Finals might have been tough, but _____
will be even harder. If you get overwhelmed, just remember to take
it one day at a time.

Pet all the dogs you can.

You're going to be great.

_____

Hey _____,

Think of this letter as the letter equivalent of a gentle poke on the shoulder.

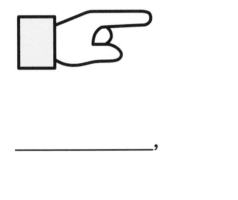

_____,

_____

Hey _____,

I wonder about you sometimes, especially because it's hard to find you on Facebook.

Do you still have that _____ laugh?

Is your hair still _____?

Do your parents still live in _____?

Did you end up becoming a _____?

Do you still love _____ the way I still do?

I hope you're good.

_____

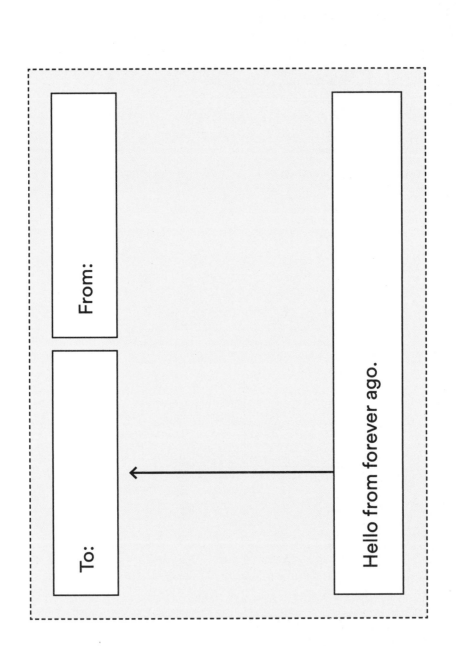

From:

To:

Hello from forever ago.

_____,

I heard that you are sick—I hope you feel

_____.

May I bring or send you . . .

◯ soup
◯ candy
◯ all of the above

. . . sometime soon?

_____

TO AN INTERNET FRIEND YOU WOULD LIKE TO GET TO KNOW BETTER

_____,

So we've been following each other on _____ for a while now. I'd like to think that we're friendly acquaintances.

But I'm wondering—do you want to be FRIENDS?

Like, we could add each other on gchat, or maybe . . . start texting?

No worries if you'd like to stick to _____. I just thought I'd, you know, ask.

_____

_____ ,

YOU CAN DO IT.

By IT, I mean _____

_____

_____ .

YOU CAN. GO.

Love,

_____

TO THE PERSON WHO LEAVES DISHES IN THE SINK

Hey _____,

The dishes in this sink—ones you got dirty—have been sitting here for __ __ days.

That's __ __ days of me barely having room to do my own dishes.

__ __ days of these dishes attracting gross bugs.

__ __ days I've had to do complicated restacking and arm gymnastics just to get a glass of water from the tap.

I want you to wash these dishes. These dishes want you to wash them. Please wash them?

Please?

_____

Dear _____,

Happy ___ ___ [st/nd/rd/th] birthday.

Of all the people who wish you happy birthday over email, Facebook, text, Twitter, Snapchat, and whatever else today, and I'm sure there will be many:

I just want to point out that I'm probably the only person who sent you a real letter. Therefore, I am the superior friend.

It's all about me, really.

(I hope you have a great day!)

Love,
_____

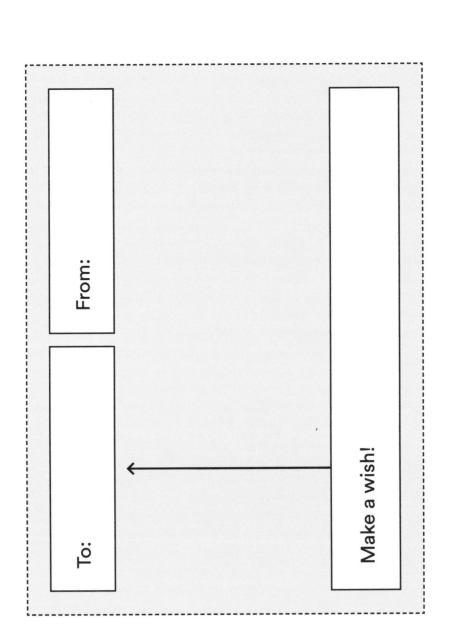

From:

To:

Make a wish!

————————————,

Congratulations on your very first job—I'm so proud of you.

You're going to hear a lot of advice about what to do and how to act and who to make connections with.

So I might as well throw my own advice on the pile, right?

Great. Here's my very best advice:

• ————————————————————.

• ————————————————————.

• ————————————————————.

• Don't hook up with anyone you work with.

• Don't hook up with anyone you work with.

That's it.

You're going to be great!

————————————

TO A FRIEND WHO'S PERPETUALLY LATE

Hey _____,

So I've noticed that you tend to be ___ ___ minutes late, like, every time we meet up. That makes me wonder a few things:

CHECK ALL THAT APPLY

___ Do you think your time is more valuable than my time?

___ Should I start to show up late—even later than you tend to— to make you wait, so you see how annoying it is?

___ Are you perpetually late because you are actually an avenging superhero of some kind and you spend your days and nights tirelessly bringing justice to those who would otherwise run free to wreak havoc on our community, terrorizing children and old ladies with impunity?

Let's talk about this the next time we meet up. I'll be there in five, just got off the train.

Love,

_____

                    ,

We're here in   .

The weather's   .

I wish you were   .

Hi _____,

I think I know what love tastes like:

It tastes like the _____
you brought me when I was [sad/angry/
frustrated] about _____.

Thank you.

_____

Hi _____,

Thank you so much for the _____ you gave me for _____. It's really _____.

I think I'll have it for a long time, and every time I look at it, I'll think of you. I definitely won't turn it into a bong.

Thanks again!

_____

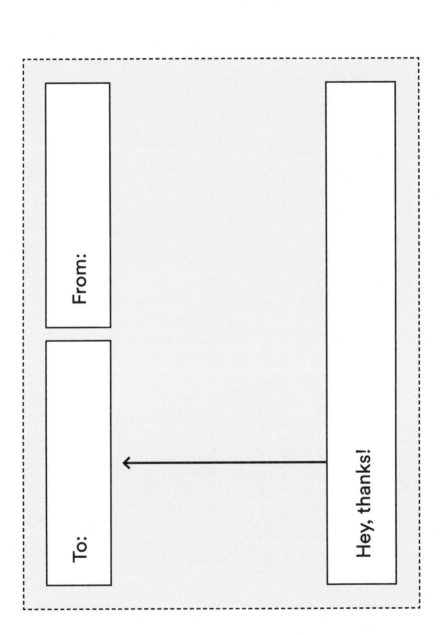

From:

To:

Hey, thanks!

TO THE PERSON WHO MYSTERIOUSLY SEEMS TO SURVIVE ONLY ON MICROWAVE POPCORN (THE NO-BUTTER, NO-SALT, LOW-FAT KIND)

Hey _____,

I don't want to butt into your dietary habits, but:

I really think you might need some protein.

(You seem a little grumpy.)

Sincerely,

_____

Dear _____,

So there's no real good way to ask this.

But last night at _____, do you happen to remember if
I maybe threw up on you?

If you need additional context, we were at _____
around __ __ : __ __ [am/pm].

This was after I was dancing on/to/with _____
and before we _____.

I'd had about __ __ shots of _____ and maybe __ __ bottles
of _____. (Give or take a few.) I think we'd just had a really
_____ conversation about _____.

The details are fuzzy.

Anyway, if I did, I am so sorry.

If I didn't, please ignore this note.

Yours,

_____

Dear _____ ,

Sorry sorry sorry sorry sorry sorry sorry sorry
sorry sorry sorry sorry sorry sorry sorry sorry
sorry sorry sorry sorry sorry sorry sorry sorry
sorry sorry sorry sorry sorry sorry sorry sorry
sorry sorry sorry sorry sorry sorry sorry sorry
sorry sorry sorry sorry sorry sorry sorry sorry
sorry sorry sorry sorry sorry sorry sorry sorry
sorry sorry sorry sorry sorry sorry sorry sorry
sorry sorry sorry sorry sorry sorry sorry sorry
sorry sorry sorry sorry sorry sorry sorry sorry
sorry sorry sorry sorry sorry sorry sorry sorry
sorry sorry sorry sorry sorry sorry sorry sorry
sorry sorry sorry sorry sorry sorry sorry.

Sincerely,

_____

TO THE PERSON YOU'RE BREAKING UP WITH (FRIENDSHIP)

_____,

It's not _____, it's _____.

_____,

_____

To coworkers

_____,

We are adults.

Adults don't need to celebrate every goddamn birthday.

Especially not with cake and, God help us, singing.

Because we are adults.

Thank you for your attention.

Sincerely,

_____

TO THE MEETING OVER-INVITER

_____ ,

Let's do a little bit of math.

The number of people you invited to the meeting:

Multiplied by how many hours the meeting was:

Multiplied by the average hourly rate those people might charge someone for their time: $.

Equals: $.

Think it'll be worth it?

——————————————,

Take your current recipient list, the one you get when you hit
"reply all" (like you usually do).

Remove everyone whose jobs you can't identify and whose
names you don't recognize.

Remove everyone who is higher up the food chain than you
and doesn't really need to know that any of this is happening,
even "for awareness" or "to be in the loop."

Remove everyone you are pointlessly trying to impress.

Remove a few more people beyond that just for good measure.

That's your recipient list.

Send.

Repeat.

Good luck.

——————————————

I lick my food.

Like, all over.

Enjoy.

————————————,

If you have something to say, here are a few direct ways you can say it (just check any and all that apply and return to me!):

☐ I disagree with your decision to _____.

☐ I think we should _____ instead.

☐ I don't like it when you _____.

☐ I think you're getting too much credit on the _____ project.

☐ I resent that you are _____ than I am.

☐ I hate your breathing guts.

Now isn't that nicer, or at least more direct?

Sincerely,

—————————————

TO THE OVERBEARING BOSS

Hi.

Remember __ __ / __ __ / __ __ __ __ ?

That was the day you hired me.

It was a good day for me. I was going to work for someone
I trusted and respected. I matched all your requirements for
_____! And you thought I did, too!

So with all due respect, I'd like to ask:
Can you let me just do my job? I know there's a lot of pressure on
you and all of us to _____.

And I get that—but I do my best work when I feel like people trust
me. When I need your help and guidance, I promise I'll ask for it.
Now here's a #1 BOSS mug for you.

_____

TO THE GUY WHO REPEATS WHAT WOMEN SAY RIGHT AFTER THEY'VE
SAID IT AND THEN GETS CREDIT FOR THEIR IDEAS BECAUSE WE LIVE
IN A PATRIARCHY AND SOMETIMES EVERYTHING IS BULLSHIT

,

We're onto you.

Signed,

Dear _____,

After _____ consideration,
I have decided to resign my position as
_____ at _____.

It has been _____
working with you and I will look back
on my time at _____ with
_____.

Sincerely,

_____

To people you know, sort of

Hi Ms./Mr. _____,

Remember me? _____, from _____ class.

It's been a while. But I was _____ the
other day and I began to think about what you taught me:

INSERT TOUCHING PERSONAL REMEMBRANCES!

You didn't just teach me _____
_____.

You taught me that _____
_____.

Thank you.

_____

TO YOUR THERAPIST

Dear _____,

So we've been seeing each other for _____.
And there's no easy way to say this.

I think we need counseling.

I mean, tell me what you think, you're the expert here.

But I can't help noticing there are a couple of things about our
relationship that are . . . maybe the right word is *problematic*:

- I'm the only one who really talks. You never tell me about how
  YOUR day went.

- Most of the time we're together, I'm lying on your couch and
  we don't even make eye contact.

- _____.

Let me know what you think.

I want to make this work.

_____

This is my pledge to you that I will not try to diagnose myself on the internet again. Ever.

I swear.

Signed,

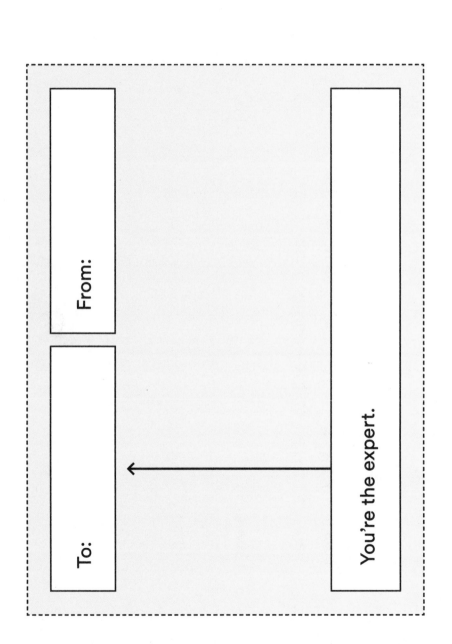

From:

To:

You're the expert.

Dear _____,

I think about this a lot:

What if you hadn't met at _____ in _____,
give or take a year?

Maybe you wouldn't have gotten together and produced
_____, who happens to be my favorite person in
the universe.

And what if you hadn't raised _____ to be kind and
_____?

What if [she/he] hadn't grown up to be _____,
_____, and _____?

I can't imagine my life without _____, exactly as
[she/he] is.

So I just want to say thank you.

_____

Dear neighbors,

We'd love it if you would stop

CHECK ALL THAT APPLY

○ parking in our spot

○ letting your dog bark for hours

○ _____

Please?

Love,
Your neighbors

Dear neighbors,

We're so sorry about

CHECK ALL THAT APPLY

◯ parking in your spot

◯ letting our dog bark for hours

◯ _____

We're doing our best not to do it again!

Love,
Your neighbors

TO YOUR POTENTIAL ROOMMATES

Hey _____,

Just wanted to say how nice it was to meet you earlier!!

I _____ the house, and everyone seems really

_____.

I know you're talking to a lot more people about the room, so just to reiterate what we talked about:

- I'm clean but not, like, a neat-freak.

- I'm super responsible but not, like, *too* responsible. I'll pay the rent on time, and I'll know what to do with a bong if you hand one to me. Unless it's a really fancy one or something.

- I'm pretty social with my roommates but I have other friends and everything. I'm not without friends. People like me.

Anyway, just wanted to make it clear that I'm really interested in the room and hope you guys pick me!!

Hope to hear from you soon!

_____

To celebrities and other abstractions

Dear God:

Please explain:

☐ the nature of love

☐ the popularity of _____

☐ that sea animal with a thing protruding from its
face that has a glowing orb at the end of it

☐ the northern lights

☐ tiny kids getting bone cancer

☐ porcupines

Looking forward to your reply.

_____

TO A CELEBRITY YOU SAW ON THE STREET

Dear _____,

Was that really you on the corner of _____
and _____ , wearing a _____ , at about
__ __ : __ __ [am/pm] last _____?

I thought you seemed . . .

CHECK ALL THAT APPLY

○ taller

○ shorter

○ older-looking

○ more dewily youthful

○ blurrily better-looking, like an out-of-focus picture

○ thirstier

○ more internet-savvy

○ kinder to animals

○ better with small children

○ more like a real person than I expected

. . . in person. That's all I really had to say.

Love, _____

Dear Tooth Fairy,

Let's talk about your per-tooth rate of compensation.
So far you've been paying me $____.____ a tooth.

But let's do some quick math here.
I'm ____ years old. On average, kids my age have ____ baby teeth.

So at $____.____ a tooth, my entire baby-tooth payout is $____.____ .

That's enough to buy a _____ , or, like, a pack of gum.
Aren't the final vestiges of my childhood worth _____ ?
Hope we can come to an understanding here.

Yours truly,

_____

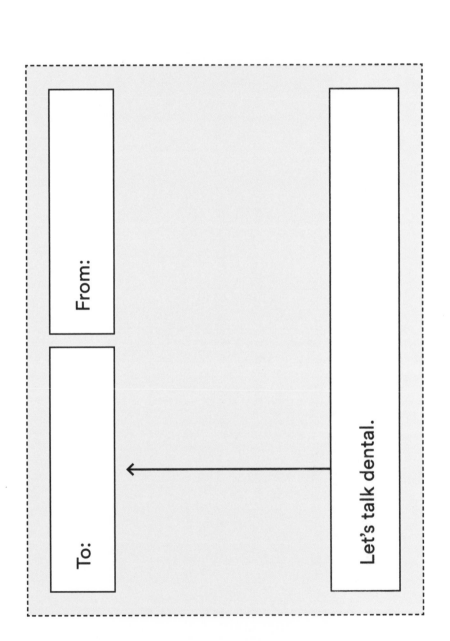

From:

To:

Let's talk dental.

Just a few things I'm saying when I hit "like":

- [ ] That's a cute baby!
- [ ] That's an ugly baby, but we're friends!
- [ ] That's a cute picture of you!
- [ ] I feel a little better about myself after seeing this picture of you!
- [ ] That's a cute picture of me!
- [ ] Happy birthday!
- [ ] OMG congrats (sincere)!
- [ ] OMG congrats (silently resentful and envious)!
- [ ] I'm going to humor this humblebrag!
- [ ] I can't stop clicking on stuff; it's like a reflex!
- [ ] You might be a person who gets me a job someday!
- [ ] You've made me appropriately nostalgic for days gone by!
- [ ] I like this!

Dear _____,

Notice me.

Notice me.

Notice me.

Notice me.

NOTICE ME.

Love,

_____

Dear Beyoncé,

Please explain:
EVERYTHING.

I want to know everything.

_____

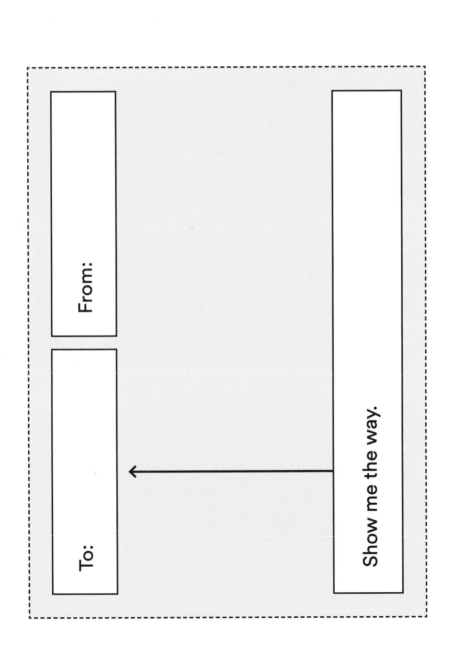

From:

To:

Show me the way.

Dear Wolf Blitzer,

Talk to me about The Situation Room.
What kinds of situations do you handle in there?

> **PLEASE GO AHEAD AND CHECK ALL THAT APPLY**

◯ serious situations

◯ vaguely humorous situations

◯ fraught situations

◯ sexy situations

◯ sad situations

◯ awkward situations

◯ furry situations

◯ moist situations

Thanks!

_____

FROM A YOUNG CHILD TO SANTA CLAUS

Dear Santa,

This year I've been:

☐ good

☐ pretty OK

☐ not great, but appropriately regretful about it, I swear

I've discussed it with my parents and all things considered I think I deserve _____ presents. Cool?

Specifically, I'd like:

• _____

• _____

• _____

Thanks. I'll be _____ next year.

Sincerely,

_____

To perfect strangers

Can you not _____?

Thanks,

The _____ who just handed
you this note.

From the _____ who just handed
you this note:

I think you're cute.

(If you're single) get in touch with me at
_____.

_____

Why

are

you

YELLING?

Hi.

Our time together will go so much better if you could just not:

☐ give your aggressive opinion on recent current events

☐ be racist

☐ be sexist

☐ try to flirt with me

Cool? Cool.

—Your passenger

It will almost certainly be fine.

TO THE PERSON IN YOUR OPPOSING POLITICAL PARTY

_____,

I think we can agree that we don't agree on:

- _____
- _____
- _____
- _____
- _____

But let's agree on one thing:

We can still be _____ without agreeing on anything.

God bless _____.

_____

TO THE PERSON WHO ASKS IF YOU'RE OKAY WHEN YOU'RE CRYING IN PUBLIC

CHECK ONE

◯ Yes, I'm okay.

◯ No, I'm not okay but I will be soon.

◯ No, I'm not okay and I'm not sure when I will be again, because have you ever actually felt like your heart was being torn apart by something? Like physically being rent in two, valves straining to hold on to their structural integrity, sinews being stretched to the limit, chamber walls expanding in a way that is unnatural and should be, because it really goddamn hurts, and you don't think you should be able to bear it as long as you can but the damn thing keeps pumping while you're in pain that you're not sure will ever end?

Thanks for asking.

_____

███████████████ ,

I have a lot of questions for you.

So do lizards run both houses of Congress?

Is lizard leadership run by consensus or, like, lizard decree?

Do the Supreme Court justices wear robes to hide the scales covering their bodies?

Is the president's human face only a mask for the lizard one hiding underneath?

What's the mechanism for getting your human face off if you have an important meeting, or you get home at the end of the day and just want to get your lizard chill on?

Why lizards and not pandas or puppies or something cuter?

Looking forward to your reply,

███████████████

Dear _____,

Here's a list of the circumstances where it's appropriate to use Comic Sans, which is a bad, clown font:

- birthday parties for kids aged nine and younger
- business dealings with bad clowns
- comics

That's the full list.

Sincerely,

_____

TO SOMEONE WHO IS WRONG ON THE INTERNET

_____,

I shouldn't be wasting my own time with this.

I shouldn't I shouldn't I shouldn't I shouldn't.

BUT:

When you said _____ on _____, I just want to make sure you know that you are utterly, totally, completely wrong for these reasons:

1. _____

2. _____

3. _____

Just so you know. You're wrong.

Sincerely,

_____

TO THE GUY STANDING NEXT TO YOU ON THE CURB AS YOU'RE WAITING

TO CROSS THE STREET WHO THINKS YOU'RE CHECKING HIM OUT WHEN

REALLY YOU'RE LOOKING TO NOT GET RUN OVER BY ONCOMING TRAFFIC

Nah, bro.

TO THE GUY WHO CATCALLS YOU

Hi from the _____ you just catcalled by saying _____
_____.

Let's do a little exercise.

First, I want you to think about every woman you've ever loved.

Your mother. Grandmother. Maybe your sister. An aunt. A great
teacher or neighbor or friend.

Maybe you once also loved a human, flesh-and-blood girlfriend or
wife and treated her kindly sometimes.

All of these women you have loved from all of these different points
in your life have one thing in common:

Every one of them has felt unsafe or _____
at one point in their lives because some asshole on the street said
_____ or did _____.

Today, for me, that asshole is you.

Sincerely,

The _____ you just catcalled

Hi.

I'm the _____ sitting __ __ row(s)
_____ you, and I can hear your
_____ from here.

So I just wanted to see if you are aware that:

- This is the Quiet Car, which attempts to be exactly what it sounds like.

- You are violating the only rule of the Quiet Car, which is that you should be quiet.

- There are __ __ other non-Quiet Cars on this train.

In the future, please try not to be an asshole.

Sincerely,

_____

Hi,

You seem very nice.

On another day, I'd want to chat with you too.

But today is not that day.

Sincerely,

[   ]

TO THE PERSON CLIPPING THEIR NAILS IN A PUBLIC PLACE

Hi from the _____ who just gave you this note.

I just wanted to talk you through something.

Think about where you are right now.

Is it:

☐ Your bathroom?

☐ Another room in your house?

☐ A bathroom somewhere else?

If you didn't check any of those boxes, it's not OK for you to be clipping your nails right now.

The more you know, right?

Stooooooooo oooooooooooooo oooooooooo
o ooooooo ooooooooooooooooooooooooo o
ooooooooooooooooooo oooooooo ooooooooo
oooo oooooooooooooooooooooooo oooooo
ooooooooooooooo oooooooooooooooooooooo
ooo oooooooooooooooooo oooo ooooooooo
oooooooooo ooooooooooooo oooooooooo
ooooooooooooooooooooooooooooooooo ooo
oooooo ooooooo ooooooooo oooooooooo
ooooooooooooooooooooo ooooooooooooooo
oo oooooooooooooooooooooooo oo oooo
ooooooo oooo ooooooooo oooooooooooooo
oooo oooooooooo oooooooooooooooooooooo
oooooooooooooooooooo oooooooooooo ooo
o ooooooooooo ooooooooo ooop.

Sincerely,

_____

TO THE PERSON ON THE AIRPLANE WHO WANTS TO TALK TO YOU

Hi _____,

To answer your questions:

I'm a _____ from _____.

Yes, it's _____ over there and the weather is _____.

I'm traveling to _____ for a _____ with my _____.

You seem very nice, and I'm sure you have a great life story.

I'm not the kind of person who chats with strangers on flights, so I hope you'll forgive me if I go back to my _____.

Have a nice trip!

Sincerely,

_____

Did you have to practice

to learn how to do that?

Did you have to practice

to learn how to do that?

I will pay you $__ __.__ __ to not come down my street again.

Hi.

I just went through _____.

I'm going to need you to take this credit card
and keep the _____ coming.

In case of inebriation so extreme I can't
stumble home, please contact _____
at _____.

Thanks,

_____

Hi!

For your reference, here is a list of circumstances in which I'd ever consider having sex with you:

THIS AREA INTENTIONALLY LEFT BLANK.

Believe it.

Best,

_____

Life templates

Dear _____,

Congratulations on your

CHECK ALL THAT APPLY

- new baby
- new job
- new house
- new pet
- promotion
- engagement
- graduation
- retirement
- birthday
- self, just generally
- hot new _____
- particularly well-filtered Instagram

I'm so happy for you.

Love,

_____

EVENT INVITE

COME TO OUR THING!

OUR THING IS A:

_____

AT THIS PLACE:

_____

ON THIS DAY:

_____

AT THIS TIME:

_____

WILL YOU COME?

◯ YES, I WILL
◯ NO, I HATE FUN

SEE YOU THERE!!

LOVE,

_____ (AND _____)

Dear _____,

_____ and _____ are thrilled to welcome our new

| CIRCLE ONE | BOY | GIRL | PUPPY |

to our home.

[She/he] arrived on _____ weighing _____, not including [booties/collar].

We've named [her/him] _____, and can't wait for you to meet [her/him].

Love from all of us,

_____

NO, THANK YOU (WITH APOLOGIES TO E. B. WHITE)

_____,

While I appreciate your invitation
to _____, I must decline,
for secret reasons.

Best regards,

_____

Dear Sirs/Madams:

I would like job, please.

Specifically, _____ at _____. Please job yes?

I look forward to hearing from you.

Sincerely,

_____

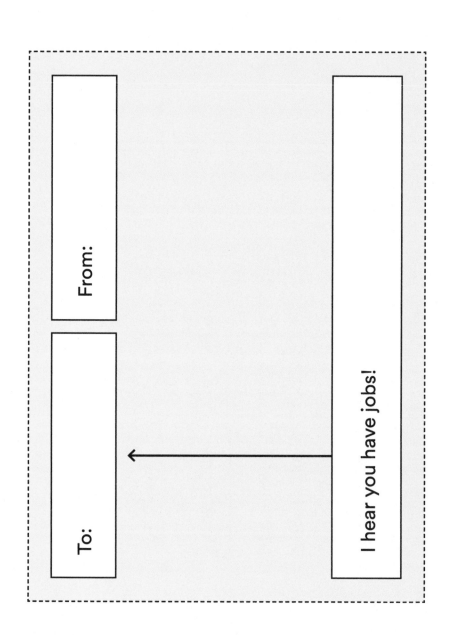

From:

To:

I hear you have jobs!

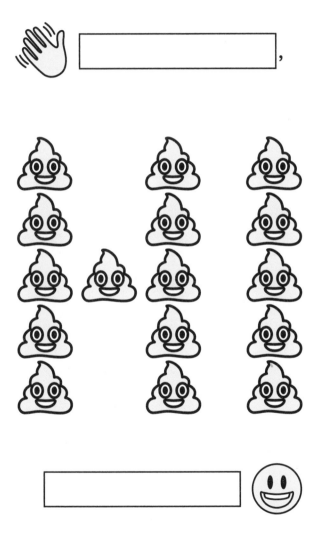

TO THE PERSON YOU NEED TO HAVE AN
UNCOMFORTABLE CONVERSATION WITH

                                     ,

I've been struggling with how to say this to you, so I'm just going to say it:

I'd love to talk to you about it more, soon. Can you let me know when you're ready?

THIS IS A CHAIN LETTER!

FORWARD THIS TO ___ ___ PEOPLE OR:

- YOUR _____ WILL FALL OUT,
- YOUR _____ WILL LEAVE YOU,
- AND YOU'LL LOSE YOUR _____.

(BASICALLY YOUR LIFE WILL BECOME A COUNTRY SONG.)

THANKS!!!!!!!

POLITICAL MISINFORMATION EMAIL FORWARD

HI. THIS MESSAGE IS OF GREAT IMPORTANCE:

DID YOU KNOW THAT _____, WHO AS
YOU KNOW IS A CANDIDATE FOR _____,
IS SECRETLY A _____ AND DEFINITELY A MENACE
TO OUR _____ AND IF NOT THAT THEN DEFINITELY A
DANGER TO EVERYTHING WE HOLD DEAR AS A CITIZENRY?

IT'S TRUE. _____ ACTUALLY *IS* A
CARD-CARRYING MEMBER OF THE _____ SOCIETY.
IT'S A REAL THING AND THEY HAVE REAL CARDS, LIKE
LAMINATED AND EVERYTHING.

IT IS CRUCIAL THAT YOU SPREAD THE WORD ABOUT THIS TO
EVERYONE YOU KNOW.

FORWARD THIS TO YOUR E-LIST NOW.

THANK YOU!!!!!!

Dear everyone who ever doubted me,

DRAW YOUR OWN OBSCENE GESTURE HERE DRAW YOUR OWN OBSCENE GESTURE HERE DRAW YOUR OWN OBSCENE GESTURE HERE DRAW YOUR OWN OBSCENE GESTURE HERE DRAW YOUR OWN OBSCENE GESTURE HERE

XO,

To everyone who would seek to curtail the rights, ambitions, or dreams of women,

Just so it's absolutely goddamn clear:

- The only person who has final say over what happens to my body is me.

- I deserve equal pay for equal work, and I'm going to get it.

- "Play like a girl" isn't an insult.

- I don't have to be pretty in order to have a right to take up space on this earth.

- I can do anything a man can. Maybe even better.

- I don't goddamn care if you like it.

Sincerely,

_____

Hey _____,

I'm so sorry for:

CHECK ALL THAT APPLY

○ hurting your feelings
○ hurting other parts of you
○ that thing that time
○ just, like, generally
○ _____

I hope you can forgive me.

Sincerely,

_____

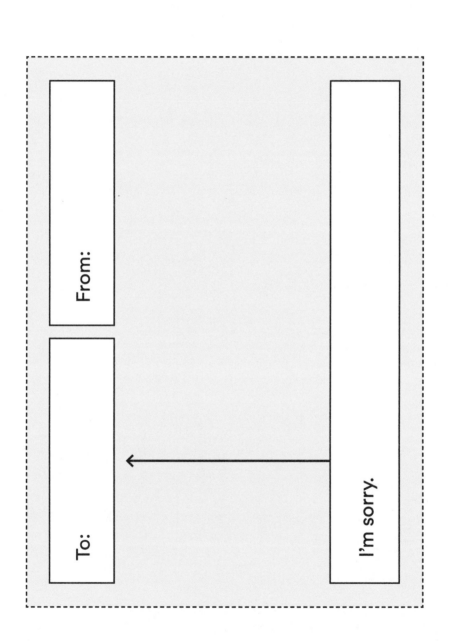

From:

To:

I'm sorry.

Dear _____:

I'd like to request a raise.

I've been in my position of _____ for ___ ___ years now,
and I've accomplished a lot:

- _____
- _____
- _____
- _____
- _____

I think an increase of my _____ salary to
$___ ___ ___ ___ ___ ___ . ___ ___ would be appropriate.

Looking forward to hearing your thoughts.

Sincerely,

_____

NOTIFICATION OF A SICK DAY

Hi _____,

I'm going to be taking a sick day today due to:

CHECK ALL THAT APPLY

- a fever
- a sore throat
- too much snot
- workplace malaise
- a generalized sense of ennui
- a really good sale at _____
- preferring to spend today hanging out with my dog
- _____

Thanks,

_____

Dear _____ ,

I recently heard about the passing of _____ and wanted
to say how very sorry I am for your loss.

_____ was _____ and _____ to me.

All my best to you and your family.

Sincerely,

_____

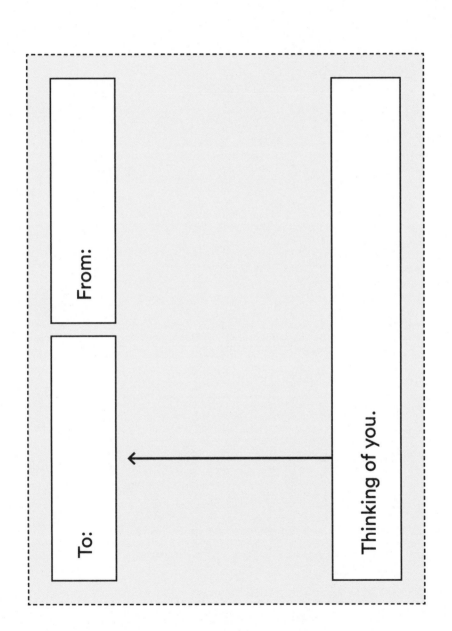

To my fans:

I could never have done it without you. All my love and galaxies of stars and sparkles and unicorns*,

[   ]

*FAME HAS MADE YOU A BIT SPACEY.**

**POSSIBLY IT IS THE DRUGS.

Dear   ,

This note is to inform you that you are an asshole for the following reasons:

And now you know.

Sincerely,

To Whom It May Concern,

I'd like to recommend _____ for _____.

_____ is:

___ conscientious
___ kind
___ friendly
___ a decent speller
___ pretty okay, despite what you might have heard elsewhere
___ not a literal shark
___ made up of carbon, oxygen, and hydrogen

I think you'd be _____ to have _____ on your
_____.

Sincerely,

_____

EXCUSE NOTE: #1

Dear _____,

Please excuse _____ for missing _____.

[She/he]

CHECK ALL THAT APPLY

○ was ill

○ had a previous engagement

○ wasn't ever gonna

I appreciate your understanding.

Sincerely,

_____

Dear _____,

Please excuse _____ from
failing to _____.

[She/he] did not want to do it.

_____,

_____

PROPOSAL

▮▮▮▮▮▮▮▮▮▮▮,

I ▮▮▮▮▮▮ you.

Will you ▮▮▮▮▮▮ me?

▮▮▮▮▮,

▮▮▮▮▮▮▮▮

Dear _____,

We're getting hitched.

Join us on _____, 20___ ___ at __ __ : __ __ [am/pm] as we promise to be nice to each other forever or at least do our very best to try and then kiss in front of our families. We would love to have you there.

RSVP

☐ Enthusiastically accept

☐ Decline with regret

Love,

_____ & _____

Dear _____,

I just wanted to say thank you for:

CHECK ALL THAT APPLY

☐ the _____ gift

☐ the _____ advice

☐ the help with _____

☐ just, like, generally

I _____ appreciate it—you're the _____.

Sincerely,

_____

Acknowledgments

Thank you to Kate McKean for suggesting that this book should exist in the first place and for guiding me through the process of making it, with occasional panic-quelling sessions at bars that serve popcorn; to Samantha Weiner, Devin Grosz, and everyone at ABRAMS for being my lovely collaborators; to my family and friends for the depth and breadth of your support, which is impossible to properly honor with words; to James, again, for good measure; and, finally, to the readers of *Everything Changes*, the newsletter that started this whole thing, for sharing your empathy and weirdness and humor with me. I am grateful.